My Brother's a Beast

Selected by
Helen Cook
and
Morag Styles

Illustrated by
Michael Charlton

The right of the
University of Cambridge
to print and sell
all manner of books
was granted by
Henry VIII in 1534.
The University has printed
and published continuously
since 1584.

ridge University Press

Cambridge
New York   Port Chester
Melbourne   Sydney

Published by the Press Syndicate of the University of Cambridge
The Pitt Building, Trumpington Street, Cambridge CB2 1RP
40 West 20th Street, New York, NY 10011-4211, USA
10 Stamford Road, Oakleigh, Melbourne 3166, Australia

This selection © Cambridge University Press 1991

Illustrations © Michael Charlton 1991

Project editor: Claire Llewellyn

First published 1991

Printed in Great Britain at the University Press, Cambridge

British Library cataloguing in publication data
My brother's a beast.
1. Poetry in English – Anthologies
I. Cook, Helen 1954–   II. Styles, Morag
821.91408

ISBN 0 521 39950 5

Acknowledgements

'Brother' by Mary Ann Hoberman, published in *Hello and Good-bye* by Little Brown. Reprinted by permission of Gina Maccoby Literary Agency. Copyright © 1959, renewed 1987 by Mary Ann Hoberman; 'I Love Me Mudder . . .' from *The Dread Affair* by Benjamin Zephaniah, Century Hutchinson; 'Wha Me Mudder Do' and 'Granny Granny Please Comb My Hair' from *Come on into My Tropical Garden* by Grace Nichols, A & C Black, 1988; 'Esme on Her Brother's Bicycle' from *The Pedalling Man* by Russell Hoban, William Heinemann Ltd; 'My Family' by Colin Finnegan from *The Skrake of Dawn*, edited by P Muldoon, Blackstaff Press; 'Winter Morning' by Frank Flynn from *The Candyfloss Tree*, Oxford University Press, 1984, reprinted by permission of the author; 'Basketball' from *Spin a Soft Black Song* by Nikki Giovanni. Copyright © 1971, 1985 by Nikki Giovanni, reprinted by permission of Farrar, Straus & Giroux, Inc.; 'Listn Big Brodda Dread, Na!' and 'Seeing Granny' from *When I Dance* by James Berry, Hamish Hamilton Ltd, 1988, London © James Berry 1988, reproduced by permission of Hamish Hamilton Ltd; 'Bedroom Skating' from *Salford Road and Other Poems* by Gareth Owen, Young Lions, 1988, reprinted by permission of the author; 'My Dad's Thumb' from *Mind Your Own Business* by Michael Rosen, André Deutsch, 1975; 'Uncle Roger' from *Nailing the Shadow* by Roger McGough (Viking Kestrel, 1987), reprinted by permission of the Peters, Fraser & Dunlop Group Ltd; extract from 'Ogun' from *The Arrivants* by Edward Kamau Brathwaite, Oxford University Press, reprinted by permission of Oxford University Press; 'Aunts and Uncles' from *A Book of Nonsense* by Mervyn Peake, Peter Owen Ltd; 'Who the Cap Fit, Let Them Wear It' from *Say it Again, Granny* by John Agard, illustrated by Susanna Gretz, The Bodley Head, 1986; 'Grandad' from *Rabbitting On* by Kit Wright, William Collins & Sons Ltd, 1978; 'Until Gran Died' from *Morning Break* by Wes Magee, Cambridge University Press, 1989, reprinted by permission of the author; 'Lineage' from *For My People* by Margaret Walker, Yale University Press, 1942 © Margaret Walker Alexander.

Every effort has been made to reach copyright holders; the publishers would be glad to hear from anyone whose rights they have unknowingly infringed.

Contents

Brother

I had a little brother
And I brought him to my mother
And I said I want another
Little brother for a change.

But she said don't be a bother
So I took him to my father
And I said this little bother
Of a brother's very strange.

But he said one little brother
Is exactly like another
And every little brother
Misbehaves a bit he said.

So I took the little bother
From my mother and my father
And I put the little bother
Of a brother back to bed.

Mary Ann Hoberman

I Love Me Mudder . . .

I love me mudder and me mudder love me
we come so far from over de sea,
we heard dat de streets were paved with gold
sometime it hot sometime it cold
I love me mudder and me mudder love me
we try fe live in harmony
you might know her as Valerie
but to me she is my mummy.

She shouts at me daddy so loud some time
she don't smoke weed she don't drink wine
she always do the best she can
she work damn hard down ina England,
she's always singing some kind of song
she have big muscles and she very very strong
she likes pussy cats and she love cashew nuts
she don't bother with no if and buts.

I love me mudder and me mudder love me
we come so far from over de sea
we heard dat de streets were paved with gold
sometime it hot sometime it cold,
I love her and she love me too
and dis is a love I know is true
me and my mudder we love you too.

Benjamin Zephaniah

Wha Me Mudder Do

Mek me tell you wha me Mudder do
wha me mudder do
wha me mudder do

Me mudder pound plantain mek fufu
Me mudder catch crab mek calaloo stew

Mek me tell you wha me mudder do
wha me mudder do
wha me mudder do

Me mudder beat hammer
Me mudder turn screw
she paint chair red
then she paint it blue

Mek me tell you wha me mudder do
wha me mudder do
wha me mudder do

Me mudder chase bad-cow
with one 'Shoo'
she paddle down river
in she own canoe
Ain't have nothing
dat me mudder can't do
Ain't have nothing
dat me mudder can't do

Mek me tell you

Grace Nichols

9

Esme on Her Brother's Bicycle

One foot on, one foot pushing, Esme starting off beside
Wheels too tall to mount astride,
Swings the off leg forward featly,
Clears the high bar nimbly, neatly,
With a concentrated frown
Bears the upper pedal down
As the lower rises, then
Brings her whole weight round again,
Leaning forward, gripping tight,
With her knuckles showing white,
Down the road goes, fast and small,
Never sitting down at all.

Russell Hoban

My Family

My dad just sits there
and reads the newspaper.
My mum is all get up and go,
My sister sits and studies all day,
My brother thinks only of football.
I often wonder what they think of me.

Mmmmmmm . . .

Colin Finnegan (aged 9)

Winter Morning

On cold winter mornings
When my breath makes me think
I'm a kettle,
Dad and me wrap up warm
In scarves and Balaclavas,
Then we fill a paper bag
With bread and go and feed the ducks
In our local park.
The lake is usually quite frozen
So the ducks can't swim,
They swim across the ice instead,
Chasing the bits of bread
That we throw,
But when they try to peck the crumbs
The pieces slip and slide away.

Poor ducks!
They sometimes chase that bread
For ages and ages,
It makes me hungry just watching them,
So when dad isn't looking
I pop some bread in my mouth and have a quick chew.
The ducks don't seem to mind,
At least they've never said anything
To me if they do.

Frank Flynn

Basketball

when spanky goes
to the playground all the big boys say
   hey big time – what's happenin'
'cause his big brother plays basketball for their
   high school
and he gives them the power sign and says
   you got it
but when i go and say
   what's the word
they just say
   your nose is running junior

one day i'll be seven feet tall
even if i never get a big brother
and i'll stuff that sweaty ball down
their laughing throats

Nikki Giovanni

14

Listn Big Brodda Dread, Na!

My sista is younga than me.
My sista outsmart five-foot three.
My sista is own car repairer
and yu nah catch me doin judo with her.

I sey I wohn get a complex.
I wohn get a complex.
Then I see the muscles my sista flex.

My sista is tops at disco dance.
My sista is well into self-reliance.
My sista plays guitar and drums
and wahn see her knock back double rums.

I sey I wohn get a complex.
I wohn get a complex.
Then I see the muscles my sista flex.

My sista doesn mind smears of grease and dirt.
My sista'll reduce yu with sheer muscle hurt.
My sista says no guy goin keep her phone-bound –
with own car mi sista is a wheel-hound.

I sey I wohn get a complex.
I wohn get a complex.
Then I see the muscles my sista flex.

James Berry

Bedroom Skating

Because there is no Ice Rink
Within fifty miles of our house,
My sister perfects her dance routines
In the Olympic Stadium of my bedroom.
Wearing a soft expression
And two big, yellow dusters on her feet,
She explodes out of cupboards
To an avalanche of music
And whirls about the polished lino
In a blur of double axels and triple salchows.
For her free-style doubles
She hurls this pillow called Torvill
From here to breakfast time
While spinning like a hippo
Round and round my bed.
Imagine waking up to that each morning;
Small wonder my hands shake
And I'm off my cornflakes.

Last Thursday she even made me
Stand up on my bed
And hold up cards marked 'Six'
While she gave victory salutes
In the direction of the gerbil's cage.
To be honest,
Despite her endless dedication
And her hours of practice
I don't think she has a hope
Of lifting the world title.
But who cares?
She may not get the gold
But I'll bet there isn't another skater alive
With wall-to-wall mirror
On her bedroom floor.

Gareth Owen

17

My Dad's Thumb

My dad's thumb
can stick pins in wood
without flinching –
it can crush family-size matchboxes
in one stroke
and lever off jam-jar lids without piercing
at the pierce here sign.

If it wanted
it could be a bath-plug
or a paint-scraper
or keyhole cover or a tap-tightener.

It's already a great nutcracker
and if it dressed
it could easily pass
as a broad bean or a big toe.

In actual fact, it's quite simply
the world's fastest envelope burster.

Michael Rosen

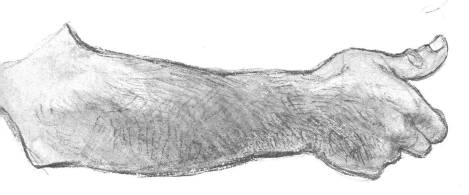

Uncle Roger

I am distinctly
ununclely.
I forget birthdays
and give Xmas presents
only when cornered.
(Money, of course, and too little.)

I am regrettably
ununclish.
Too thin to be jolly,
I can never remember
jokes or riddles.
Even fluff
my own poems.

My nephews and nieces
as far as I know
disuncled
me some time ago.
Better uncleless
than my brand of petty
uncleness.

Roger McGough

EXTRACT FROM **Ogun**

My uncle made chairs, tables, balanced doors on, dug out
coffins, smoothing the white wood out

with plane and quick sandpaper until
it shone like his short-sighted glasses.

The knuckles of his hands were sil-
vered knobs of nails hit, hurt and flat-

tened out with blast of heavy hammer. He was
knock-knee'd, flat-
footed and his clop clop sandals slapped across the concrete

flooring of his little shop where canefield mulemen and a fleet
of Bedford lorry drivers dropped in to scratch themselves
and talk.

There was no shock of wood, no beam
of light mahogany his saw teeth couldn't handle.

When shaping squares for locks, a key hole
care tapped rat tat tat upon the handle

of his humpbacked chisel. Cold
world of wood caught fire as he whittled: rectangle

window frames, the intersecting x of fold-
ing chairs, triangle

trellises, the donkey
box-cart in its squeaking square.

Edward Kamau Brathwaite

Aunts and Uncles

When Aunty Jane
Became a Crane
She put one leg behind her head;
And even when the clock struck ten
Refused to go to bed.

When Aunty Grace
Became a Plaice
She all but vanished sideways on;
Except her nose
And pointed toes
The rest of her was gone.

When Aunty Jill
Became a Pill
She stared all day through dark-blue glass;
And always sneered
When men appeared
To ask her how she was.

When Uncle Jake
Became a Snake
He never found it out;
And so as no one mentions it
One sees him still about.

Mervyn Peake

My Aunt She Died a Month Ago

My aunt she died a month ago,
And left me all her riches,
A feather-bed and a wooden leg,
And a pair of calico breeches;
A coffee pot without a spout,
A mug without a handle,
A baccy box without a lid,
And half a farthing candle.

Anon

Who the Cap Fit, Let Them Wear It

If it wasn't you
who tek de chalk
and mark up de wall
juggle with de egg
and mek it fall
then why you didn't answer
when you hear Granny call?

If it wasn't you
who bounce yuh ball
in de goldfish bowl
wipe mud from yuh shoes
all over the floor
and poke yuh finger
straight in de butter

If it wasn't you
then why yuh heart a-flutter?
why yuh voice a-stutter?
and why you look so jumpy
when you stand up in front of Granny?

who the cap fit,
let dem wear it.
That's what Granny does always say
and that she wasn't born yesterday.

John Agard

Grandad

*Grandad's dead
And I'm sorry about that.*

He'd a huge black overcoat.
He felt proud in it.
You could have hidden
A football crowd in it.
Far too big –
It was a lousy fit
But Grandad didn't
Mind a bit.
He wore it all winter
With a squashed black hat.

Now he's dead
And I'm sorry about that.

He'd got twelve stories.
I'd heard every one of them
Hundreds of times
But that was the fun of them:
You knew what was coming
So you could join in.
He'd got big hands
And brown, grooved skin
And when he laughed
It knocked you flat.

Now he's dead
And I'm sorry about that.

Kit Wright

Granny Granny Please Comb My Hair

Granny Granny
please comb my hair
you always take your time
you always take such care

You put me to sit on a cushion
between your knees
you rub a little coconut oil
parting gentle as a breeze

Mummy Mummy
she's always in a hurry-hurry
rush
she pulls my hair
sometimes she tugs

But Granny
you have all the time in the world
and when you're finished
you always turn my head and say
'Now who's a nice girl.'

Grace Nichols

Seeing Granny

Toothless, she kisses
with fleshly lips
rounded, like mouth
of a bottle, all wet.

She bruises your face
almost, with two
loving tree-root hands.

She makes you sit, fixed.
She then stuffs you
with boiled pudding and lemonade.

She watches you feed
on her food. She milks
you dry of answers
about the goat she gave you.

James Berry

Until Gran Died

The minnows I caught
lived for a few days in a jar
then floated side-up on the surface.
We buried them beneath the hedge.
I didn't cry, but felt sad inside.

I thought
I could deal with funerals,
that is until Gran died.

The goldfish I kept in a bowl
passed away with old age.
Mum wrapped him in newspaper
and we buried him next to a rose bush.
I didn't cry, but felt sad inside.

I thought
I could deal with funerals
that is until Gran died.

My cat lay stiff in a shoe box
after being hit by a car.
Dad dug a hole and we buried her
under the apple tree.
I didn't cry, but felt *very* sad inside.

I thought
I could deal with funerals,
that is until Gran died.

And when she died
I went to the funeral
with relations dressed in black.
They cried, and so did I.
Salty tears ran down my face. Oh, how I cried.

Yes, I thought
I could deal with funerals,
that is until Gran died.

She was buried in a graveyard
and even the sky wept that day.
Rain fell and fell and fell,
and thunder sobbed far away across the town.
I cried and I cried.

I thought
I could deal with funerals,
that is until Gran
died.
Wes Magee

Lineage

My grandmothers were strong.
They followed plows and bent to toil.
They moved through fields sowing seed.

They touched earth and grain grew.
They were full of sturdiness and singing.
My grandmothers were strong.

My grandmothers are full of memories.
Smelling of soap and onions and wet clay
With veins rolling roughly over quick hands
They have many clean words to say.
My grandmothers were strong.
Why am I not as they?

Margaret Walker